Cc

MW01520045

TRAVEL GUIDE

FOR

2023, 2024,

AND BEYOND

A Guidebook to this Beautiful Country

ALEXANDER HARRIS

TABLE OF CONTENTS

INTRODUCTION
TO COSTA RICA

Costa Rica is truly such an amazing country. With an abundance of wildlife, magical waterfalls, and a laid-back community, it is no wonder that this is a major destination for travelers. Throughout this guide, you'll find information on everything like how to get around in the country, best places to visit, the most delicious foods to try, what to pack for certain activities, and so much more. Plus, there are also great recommendations by fellow travelers (including the one writing this guide) to make your trip a breeze!

So sit back, get your reading glasses on, and prepare for the Pura Vida as an unforgettable travel experience awaits!

WHAT TO KNOW
BEFORE VISITING

Before you enter any country, it is important to, of course, do some research. No traveler should ever enter a new territory without having some background knowledge. We've narrowed down a couple of key points for you to have in mind before visiting Costa Rica.

- The capital of Costa Rica is San José.
  - If you're flying into the country, this is most likely the place where you will land. In full transparency, travelers do not spend too much time in the capital (unless you're a history buff, which in that case, there is a section for you later on in this guide). At the airport, you'll probably see tourists going immediately for the public buses or private shuttles to visit the destinations of their choice.

- Costa Rica is divided into 7 provinces:
  - ○ Alajuela
  - ○ Cartago
  - ○ Guanacaste
  - ○ Heredia
  - ○ Limon
  - ○ Puntarenas
  - ○ San José

- The currency that is used in Costa Rica is the Costa Rican Colón. This is used in all parts of the country.
  - ○ 1 CRC = 0.0017 USD
  - ○ 1 USD = 584.32 CRC

- The official national language of Costa Rica is Spanish.
  - ○ As a visitor to any country, it is important to learn at least the basics of the language out of respect. If you're behind on your Spanish, don't freak out just yet. Costa Rica is a major tourist destination, so English is spoken in many towns. But, if you are interested in having a deeper dive with the language, please make sure to check out the following programs:

- Duolingo (Free and short lessons given through a phone application)

- Rosetta Stone (Usually provided for free by your local library and in our opinion, one of the best methods to learn a new language)

- Fluent Forever (Created by an opera singer who is fluent in 7 languages, this app has a 2-week trial and so many helpful language learning methods through their website)

- Spanish Hours (YouTube channel with super helpful videos)

- Babbel (Inexpensive lessons that provide lectures through reading, writing, listening, and speaking)

○ A term that you won't find in your Spanish lessons is "Tico" or "Tica." This means someone who is native to Costa Rica. Nicaragua does the same with "Nica/Nico."

- On the topic of being a major tourist destination, please expect areas full of immigrants (mainly from America) and not locals. The Costa Rican government allows for people to stay up to 90 days without a Visa, so many times, people will cross one of the borders to either Nicaragua or Panama and come back into the country. You will see many people working remotely, volunteering, teaching surf lessons, leading yoga retreats, etc. If you're looking for a cultural immersion in Central America, Costa Rica is probably not the best destination for that experience.

- The population of Costa Rica is about 5.2 million (San José having the highest population of 333,980) and the median age is 33.5 years.

- The Pacific coast and Caribbean coasts are very different. The west coast of the country is more for partying and surfing, while the east coast is more for chilling and relaxing. There's also a huge cultural difference and you'll notice how activities vary depending on the coast. Our recommendation is to make a trip to both coasts to see what you like, because you never know until you try.

- When you arrive in a town, you are going to see so many touring agencies. It may feel a little overwhelming having the travel agents in your face, but at the end of the day, it's their job. It may look like a scam at times, but honestly, pay for the tour. It's so worth experiencing a part of the country from a local's perspective.

- Compared to the other countries located in Central America, Costa Rica is the most expensive. In fact, for backpackers going through the Americas, it is wise to usually spend less time in Costa Rica compared to the other countries. Some people compare the prices to what they would spend in many areas of the US. Here are average prices of what a traveler would typically spend in a day in Costa Rica:

  - ○ Breakfast - 4000 CRC
  - ○ Lunch - 7000 CRC
  - ○ Dinner - 12000 CRC
  - ○ Tour - 23000 CRC
  - ○ Smoothie - 800 CRC
  - ○ Bike Rental (Daily) - 12000 CRC
  - ○ Beer - 1100 CRC Cocktail - 1700 CRC (More expensive in large restaurants)
  - ○ Average total per day - 61600 CRC

- In the prime age of technology, we use our phones to guide us in the right direction. With that being said, how will we use our maps without a signal in Costa Rica? First things first, if you have an international plan, you're set. If you are looking for something a bit more economical, you can also get a SIM card when you're in the country. These typically cost around 2000 CRC + any additional money for internet and phone services. There are also apps that work really well for people who don't want to use their cellular data:

- ○ Google Maps (You can download a map for a specific region and use it offline)
- ○ Maps.Me (Very easy map that is popular among many travelers and includes offline maps)
- ○ Waze (Set a destination and Waze will take you there. Plus, there is no internet connection needed)

● As for safety, just like any other country that you will visit, just be aware of your surroundings and don't flaunt luxury goods. Travelers do feel safe in Costa Rica, but that doesn't mean that you should be completely unaware of everything going on. Please make sure that your possessions are with you at all times, your money is located in a purse in front of you, and that you do not wander around late at night by yourself.

● Costa Rica is a beautiful country with natural landscapes like the beach or the mountains that you have probably never seen before. This travel guide will provide you with more details on the biodiversity of this country, but in the meantime, here are some fun facts for you to keep in mind:

- ○ Costa Rica is one of the most welcoming countries in the world. Tourists are very much welcomed and there is barely any discrimination.
- ○ The Costa Rican Cólon is colorful with red, blue, yellow, and green colors.
- ○ There are 6 active volcanoes and 61 dormant volcanoes.
- ○ Costa Rica is home to over 500,000 different wildlife species.
- ○ Turn on the radio every morning and you will hear the national anthem.

- ● You're going to hear "Pura Vida" all throughout Costa Rica, but what does it mean? To provide a direct translation, it means "pure life," aka a simple way of living. It radiates good, easy, and friendly energy throughout the country. It can also serve as a variety of responses. A common one is when someone sees you stressed, they'll mention "Pura Vida" for you to calm down.

BEST TIMES TO VISIT

*Q*uick preview: Before diving into this section, it is good to have some prior knowledge of what type of environments will be mentioned.

● *Tropical Country*

○ *A tropical country lies within the "tropics" region, which is in the Tropics of Cancer. The equator is located at the center of the tropics making the weather typically warm all year round. It also tends to receive an abundance of rainfall.*

● *Dry Season*

○ *Dry season is associated with tropical countries and is a period of low rainfall. There are typically high temperatures during this time and low humidity due to the lack of rain.*

When you're on TikTok and type in "Costa Rica" in the search bar, you're going to see gorgeous beaches and beautiful tropical landscapes. It is true that Costa Rica has pretty consistent weather throughout the year. The country's annual temperature can range from 75 to 90 degrees Fahrenheit, making it the perfect vacation spot all year round.

There are months that do have more rainfall than the others, and they are from May to December. But don't let rain discourage you from traveling to Costa Rica. This only enhances your trip experience by allowing you to see vibrant green, natural views. In reality, what you plan on doing will be dependent on the time you go.

Here are some tips for planning accordingly for your Costa Rica trip:

- Remember that Costa Rica is a tropical country. Therefore, the weather can be quite unpredictable. According to multiple travel bloggers, December to April has the most stable weather and is probably the most popular time to visit.

- During March, the country is quite busy with many tourists, especially those trying to escape the cold. So, if you want a relaxing break, be sure to avoid this hectic month and head to Costa Rica during May and June for a more calming experience.

- Dry season begins around November/December. If you don't want the rain to put a halt to any activities, be sure to visit during this time period.

- If you're looking for a cultural experience and want to be in the country when major events happen, be sure to visit during April for Semana Santa, or Easter holy week. If you've been to Latin America, then you know that this week is no joke. Holy Thursday, Good Friday, and Easter Sunday will have town gatherings with flamboyant events. It's definitely something that every traveler should experience! Also, did you know that Costa Rica has Carnival? In Puerto Limon, Carnival is held in October and celebrates the huge Afro-Caribbean community. There are colorful costumes, delicious Caribbean food, and lots of reggae music.

People from all over the world come to experience Costa Rica's glorious weather, and according to *Statista*, the United States seems to be the country where most tourists come from. This is true for many Central American countries considering the proximity to the States. Canada is next in line, and visitors do tend to come when the snow begins to hit. Mexico is next on the list due to its proximity.

WHAT TO PACK
FOR YOUR TRIP

L ater on in the guide, you'll find mini packing lists based off of locations and activities. The items will typically be accompanied with detailed descriptions and reasons why you should bring them. This list serves as a general overview and one that you could consistently refer off of. In addition to clothes and toiletries, you should bring:

- ● Sunscreen
- ● Mosquito repellent
- ● Rain jacket
- ● Hiking shoes
- ● Sunglasses and hat
- ● Water shoes
- ● Rash guard shirt
- ● Towels

- Umbrella
- Tote bag
- Swimsuit
- Mini first-aid kit

Now, we can't include a packing list in a travel guide without recommending which types of bags to take. Unless you're going to a luxurious resort, make sure to pack light and use small luggage for Costa Rica. The reason why is because to get to your destination, (and assuming that you won't be taking a private shuttle), you're most likely going to drag your luggage to get to your hotel and toss it behind a motor vehicle. It is recommended to NOT bring bags with wheels just because if you go to a beach town, the roads sometimes aren't paved. Trust us when we say that dragging luggage with wheels on a dirt road is not ideal. If you're moving around the country very often and planning on crossing a border to another, then it's recommended that you bring one of the big, typical backpacker bags. This will make your life easier as you often have to transfer buses when crossing a border.

Please find some luggage and bag recommendations below:

For those of you staying at a resort or designated area, and are not hopping from place to place:

- Main Luggage & Carry-On Options
  - *Please note that these pieces of luggage are at a higher price point, and there are dupes found online. These brands and pieces are recommended due to their credibility and great customer reviews.*

  - Briggs & Riley
    - This is a luxury luggage brand with a lifetime guarantee. Their International Carry-On Spinner is perfect for any country!

  - Calpak
    - Calpak has been becoming more and more popular all over social media. Their Ambeur Medium Luggage is very spacious and serves as a great main luggage.

  - Away
    - Away is honestly for the millennial and younger traveler. Their Carry-on Flex seems to be one of the most popular items that easily sells out on their website.

- Bag (to bring in the airplane seat with you)

  - Béis - Mini Weekender

    - Béis is honestly a brand for the corporate girlies. The celebrity-owned brand is super stylish and caters to so many travel needs. The Mini Weekender in particular is a spacious and very classy bag. There is also a Convertible option which allows you to remove the bottom portion as needed.

  - Cotopaxi - Allpa 35L

    - If you want something that's more of a backpack style, check out Cotopaxi. They have some great options, and the Allpa 35L seems to be the most popular choice for packing light. You can also carry it like a suitcase.

  - Peak Design - Travel Backpack 45L

    - With many storage pockets and 360 grab handles, this Peak Design Backpack has been awarded numerous times. Plus, it has a lifetime guarantee.

For those of you who are planning on doing more of a backpacking trip, here are some great options for larger backpacks:

- Granite Gear Blaze 60

  - This backpack is great for people who tend to overpack. Not only is it spacious, but the material allows it to carry any load.

- Osprey Aether 65

  - This bag can also take on heavier loads and seems to be commonly used by many backpackers.

- High Sierra Pathway 2.0 60L Backpack

  - This backpack has a variety of compartments, which makes it great for those who really like to stay organized while they travel.

Here are some more items that we think you should bring along on your trip, which can all be purchased on Amazon.

- Packing Cubes

  - Not only will these help you stay organized, but packing cubes allow you to save space in any luggage. They also allow

16

you to keep your clothes in nicer conditions.

● Portable Charger

  ○ A portable charger and cord are always great items to have when you're traveling. You may be taking more photos than usual, and using your maps often, so best to have a power source for emergencies.

● Reusable Water Bottle

  ○ You should be avoiding any type of plastic in Costa Rica. Make sure to bring your own bottle along with you or purchase one in the country.

● Microfiber Towel

  ○ A microfiber towel is small and compact, making it perfect for any trip. Our recommendation is to bring two of them with you—one for showering and the other for any beach activities.

HOW TO GET
AROUND IN COSTA RICA

Getting around Costa Rica can be a significant challenge, especially when you are the one driving. Filled with potholes and tricky routes, the road is unsafe for tourists. Therefore, renting a vehicle is not highly recommended. However, a better alternative would be to hire a car-and-driver service (recommended by your hotel). So now, you can enjoy the beautiful scenery without worrying about the road.

Having your personal driver can be pricey, especially if you are on a budget. Expect to pay at least $100 per day. Some hotels offer a car-and-driver service. Car-and-driver services allow you to travel the country with a driver. Some authorized drivers provide information on the country throughout the trip. Costa Rica Driver, Gray Line, Tours By Locals, and Tropical Tours Shuttles are all certified car driver companies.

Another option to consider while planning your trip to Costa Rica is taking buses. The bus is the cheapest and most reliable way to get around the country. It runs on a schedule and takes you through the capital. However, the bus has a notable drawback, speed. A one-hour flight on a plane may take the bus nine hours to arrive. Therefore, it is recommended that you use the bus for shorter trips around the city. There are also private bus shuttles that work with tourists.

Taking a taxi is also a good form of transportation for your trip. Before you use a taxi, negotiate with the cab driver about the trip's price. Also, please keep in mind that Uber only works in some cities and primarily in the capital San José (and so does Uber Eats).

When you're settled in the town/area of your choice, the main method of transportation will most likely be walking. This is normal in many coastal towns, and you'll see locals and tourists doing so. If things are a bit more far apart, consider renting a moped, just like you've probably seen those YouTube couples go around the country with. They're very common in Costa Rica and extremely easy to rent (or if you want to stay longer, then buy one). If you're in rougher terrain, you'll have the option to rent an RTV vehicle. This is very common in Santa Teresa, and some even argue that it's easier to navigate than a moped.

We understand that renting a moped may still frighten some people. Another option is an electric scooter. They don't go as quickly as mopeds do and come out to a cheaper price to rent. Plus, if you run out of gas, you're able to pedal all the way back home.

If you are on a budget, then bikes are the best method of transportation. In fact, when you enter a coastal town, you'll notice that many people are riding bikes, so it will probably convince you to get one asap. When you rent one, the rental places usually provide you with a lock and key.

We'll have recommended transportation rental locations once we get into detail of the best places to visit in Costa Rica.

EATING AND
DRINKING IN COSTA RICA

If you walk into a restaurant in Costa Rica and ask what you should have, the waiter is immediately going to tell you the Casado. You may then develop a confused look on your face because if you remember from your Duolingo lesson, "casado" means "married" in Spanish. While this does ring true in the romance language, the Casado is a Costa Rican meal that consists of rice, meat, beans, vegetables, plantains, and tortilla. In some restaurants, they even serve it with a fried egg if you would like (and highly recommended for the delicious blend of flavors). In addition to the traditional Casado, Costa Rica has a variety of mouthwatering foods to fuel your energy levels while visiting the country.

Similar to their neighbor Nicaragua, Gallo Pinto is a popular dish and consists of rice and beans. Now, this may sound a bit dull when you first hear it (especially considering that it is literally called "painted rooster" in

Spanish), but this dish serves as a base. The rice and beans are full of seasoning, and you can accompany Gallo Pinto with meat, eggs, tortillas, etc. This is typically what is eaten during breakfast and served with cheese, egg, and a nice coffee. It's a great way to get protein as well as feeling satisfied with the rice.

Another dish definitely worth mentioning is the "palm of heart" or the "Palmito" (yet another Spanish word with a different meaning). Palmitos come from (you guessed it) the heart of a peach palm tree, also referred to as Pejibaye. There are many ways that you would typically eat Palmito in Costa Rica. You can have it with rice, salad, or even in soup if you want something a bit cozy. However you decide to have it, these palm hearts will definitely leave you craving more!

Something that tourists typically don't have when visiting Costa Rica is the Olla de Carne. Considering that it is a stew, most tourists would typically ask for something a bit less warm. But in full transparency, this rich and hearty meal will leave you craving more. It contains slowly-cooked beef, corn, carrots, and so many more vegetables. If you're ever craving something cozy, this is definitely the go-to.

Empanadas are all over Latin America, but they are all different in each country. If you don't know what they are, they are fried dough stuffed with delicious ingredients of your choice. Dominicans will typically make their empanadas with beef and raisins. Colombians will have corn dough as their base and stuff potatoes inside. Costa Ricans also use corn dough and fill their empanadas with any food of choice. There are options for sweet or savory ones. A highly recommended empanada is "arregladas" which is full of mayonnaise, ketchup, and cabbage salad (yum). Despite being extremely tasty, the reason why empanadas are mentioned in this travel guide is because you don't need to sit at a restaurant to enjoy them. If you're looking for something quick and to-go, empanadas are the perfect option. Many cafes have them, and you'll even see food stands with people selling them. Get them while they're hot!

If you're craving something sweet, then Costa Rica is your spot, especially considering the amount of sugar cane in the country. While you can taste a bit of every dessert, Tres Leches is considered to be the national dessert of Costa Rica. If you're not familiar with this decadent dessert, it's basically a sponge cake full of three milks (aka tres leches). There are also fruit-filled empanadas, arroz con leche, miel de coco and so much more.

Something else that may be popular for sweet-toothed mongers and for those above the legal drinking age is Guaro. Guaro is a sugar cane-based liquor and sold throughout the country. The bartenders can definitely get creative with this drink and include lime juice, mint, etc. It's definitely something worth trying and experimenting different cocktails with.

Fun tip: If you're not a fan of liquor and would rather lean more toward beer, then Imperial, Costa Rica's national beer, is for you.

We definitely can't speak about Costa Rican food without mentioning the fruits. There's something for everyone all year round! Of course, you're going to want a coconut and enjoy the Pura Vida while lying on the beach, but you can't miss out on all the fruits that you'll find. There are pitahayas, breadfruit, mangoes, guanabanas, and so much more! You can find these of course in markets, but the best fruits of course come from roadside stands. The vendors will give you a good deal and even cut/peel the fruit for you.

Now if you've been on Instagram, you'll notice all the smoothies and fruit bowls that Costa Rica has to offer. It is always great to get a taste of the blend of natural flavors. Just like the fruits, you are able to receive them at fruit vendors. Cafes are also great spots to just relax and enjoy the aesthetically-pleasing smoothie bowls.

While tipping isn't as huge as in the United States, it is polite to leave an amount for waiters at restaurants. Since so many tourists visit, it is the least we could do for those consistently catering to foreigners.

Another quick tip for Costa Rica. No need to invest in water bottles. The tap water is safe to drink in the country. Of course, just like any other country, be a bit more wary of drinkable water in rural areas—you may want to bring a water bottle there. Also, if you do have a sensitive stomach, a life straw or water bottle would probably be the best option.

Just like every country, there are many cultural influences. On the east coast, especially in the Limon province, you'll find laid-back Caribbean vibes. While traditional Costa Rica food is prominent, there is also flavorful Caribbean food worth noting. Some dishes that you'll have are coconut rice, stew chicken, and fried plantains. If you end up visiting Puerto Viejo, a highly recommended restaurant is *Reggae Chill*. It's right in front of the beach and the perfect lunch spot. Upon entering, you smell the delicious cuisine and just sit back and "chill." There is flavorful Jamaican-inspired food that will fill you up after your excursions. Plus, their lime juice is the best reward after a long bike ride in the Caribbean sun.

More recommended restaurants are to come later on in the guide!

ACCOMMODATION
IN COSTA RICA

There are a variety of places to stay all around Costa Rica. Whether you're looking for a hostel, hotel, or luxurious resort, Costa Rica has something for everybody. If you want something with a 360 view of greenery, Costa Rica has it. If you're looking for something a bit more isolated and quiet, Costa Rica has it. If you're a backpacker looking for a hostel, you guessed it, Costa Rica has it!

While a more detailed guide on location awaits, here are some tips that will help with your booking.

- Remember to book in advance for Costa Rica, especially if you're a backpacker that sort of "goes with the flow." As previously mentioned, Costa Rica is the most visited country in Central America, meaning that a lot of places go fast. If you've ever backpacked throughout Central America, you know that solo travelers heading to

Costa Rica do NOT play games when it comes to booking a place.

- ○ We know that it can also be overwhelming to find shelter, so here are some of the best websites to find accommodations:

    - ■ Booking.com (Great for finding apartments, hotel rooms, hostels, etc. Plus, it's pretty easy to get to the level to receive 10% off your booking)

    - ■ Hostelworld (One of the top websites to find hostels)

    - ■ Airbnb (Great for those who want more of a house and typically have a larger group)

    - ■ Expedia

    - ■ Hotwire

● Did you know that hostels allow you to stay for free if you volunteer? That's right! If you contact one of the hostel owners and express your interest in volunteering for a certain period of time, they will consider you as a part of the hostel team. Tasks and duties include checking people in at reception, hosting events, decorating, etc.

It's also a great experience to go through because you just end up meeting SO MANY people from all over the world. Of course, remember to apply on time to ensure a volunteer spot.

● If you are on a budget, be sure to find accommodations that include breakfast. As you now know, Costa Rican breakfast can really fill you up (assuming that your meal will most likely be Gallo Pinto). You'll have a hearty meal for your excursions for free.

● Another great tip is to make sure that you check out and establish the activities that you would like to do way before booking. For instance, you may come across a beautiful cabin in the middle of Costa Rica's vibrant greenery, but wait one second. Are you interested in doing anything in that area? A good way to determine this is to look at activities based on the area that you want to go to, which we will learn more about in the next section.

WHERE TO GO
AND WHAT TO DO

So now that you have a general introduction to Costa Rica, it's time to go into detail about what you could possibly do there in what region. There is just so much to do in Costa Rica! Whether you're looking for outdoor adventure or week-long yoga retreats, there's something for everyone!

SAN JOSÉ

Let's begin with San José, since this is the starting point for many travelers (since they usually fly in through San José Airport). Many people immediately leave the capital to visit all of the Instagram, nature-esque spots around the country. But you can definitely see a good amount in San José if you stay for at least a day.

Now, as previously mentioned, it's important to learn about a country before visiting. Some people are specifically interested in exploring history. While Costa

Rica is usually known for the fun activities, there are many museums and tours that one could attend to learn about the country's rich history. Most of these historical sites are located in the capital, just like any other city.

Things to Do:

- Learn at Museums
  - Museo Nacional de Costa Rica
    - This is the perfect place to get an overview of Costa Rica's history. It includes many exhibits that may catch your attention.
  - Museo del Jade
    - This museum shows the archaeology of Costa Rica.
  - Pre-Columbian Gold Museum
    - Any gold museum tour in Latin America is just so cool! It's also a great chance to learn about the Indigenous people in that area.
- Take Day Trips
  - If you do decide to spend your time in San José, you have many options for

amazing day trips. Check out some great options below:

- ■ Poas Volcano National Park

    - ● Poas volcano erupted a couple of times in 2017 and didn't reopen until the following year. You can either get there by driving, public bus (most affordable option and what travelers usually lean toward), or private shuttle. It is quite a walk once you get to the area, so you do have to watch a safety video before entering. It also is a cold area and does tend to rain, so be prepared for that.

- ■ Cartago

    - ● Cartago is the former capital of Costa Rica and only a 30-minute drive away. It has many historical sights to see. Also, the Central Market there is a great place for handcrafted souvenirs (it's open on Thursdays and Saturdays).

- **■ Irazú Volcano**

  - ● This is one of the most active volcanoes in Costa Rica and also happens to be the tallest. If you're brave enough and decide to hike this volcano, you will probably have the best view in the whole country! It's about an hour away from San José.

Where to Stay:

- ● Capital Hostel de Ciudad

  - ○ This is a very quiet and laid-back hostel. It is also probably one of the cleanest hostels you will ever encounter on your backpacking trip.

- ● Grano de Oro

  - ○ This hotel and restaurant fusion is top-rated in Costa Rica. You can eat inside the elegant dining area or in the romantic courtyard. The inside has the traditional tables and chairs neatly prepared. Outside, there is a fountain in the middle of the yard with red-clothed tables under patio umbrellas surrounding it.

- <u>Hotel Barceló San José</u>

Where and What to Eat:

- If you're seeking that cultural experience, then go to the San José Central Market to have breakfast or lunch. They sell everything there and even include restaurants for people to stop and enjoy a bite. You'll have a traditional meal with locals. While you're there, you may also encounter Lola Mora's Ice Cream and if you do, then you HAVE to stop by! This is Costa Rica's homemade ice cream made with only natural ingredients. It's definitely worth a visit!

- If you do want to eat at some different restaurants, here are some top choices:

  - Bacchus

  - La Divina Comida (Peruvian fusion)

  - Furca

How to Get Around:

- Just like any other capital city, Uber works in San José. Another way that many people typically get around is by taking the public city bus. It's fast, easy, and fairly priced.

- As you're looking to leave the capital, consider taking a private or public bus for your next destination.

MONTEVERDE

Monteverde is next on our sample itinerary. It's a town located in the Puntarenas province, and it is considered to be the country's cloud forest. Let's get into it.

Things to Do:

- Zipline through Lush Tropical Rainforests, aka, the Cloud Forest

  - When people mention Costa Rica, it's usually accompanied by their desire to go ziplining, and Monteverde is apparently known as the birthplace of ziplining. There are many guided circuits that take you through incredible locations. A recommended company is The Original Canopy Tour Monteverde. They offer packages with additional fun activities.

  - Here's what you need to go ziplining in Monteverde or any part of the country:

■ Note that all equipment (harness, helmet, etc.) will be provided by the travel company that you decide to go with.

■ Bring Comfortable Clothes

- You're going to have a harness strapped throughout different parts of your body for a couple of hours, so it's best to be as comfortable as possible. Considering Costa Rica's tropical weather, be sure to wear breathable clothes.

■ Wear Sneakers

- Ziplining companies will not allow you to participate in the activity without shoes that tie or strap on because you could easily lose one of them if otherwise.

■ Avoid Unnecessary Garments

- Anything like jewelry, scarves, hats, etc., can be left in your hotel room. These are items that can easily fall off during the fast adventure.

- If you want to bring a camera or phone for communication and of course pictures, that's completely fine. Just be sure to communicate that with the ziplining guide taking you through the route. Many times, the guide will hold this for you in one of their pouches and even provide you with photos/videos.

- Experience the Cloud Forest

  ○ The Monteverde Cloud Forest Biological Preserve will have you feeling like you can touch the clouds—literally! At this park, you're able to take a guided tour, take a walk on your own, and even stay overnight. This is certainly an experience that everyone has to see when they visit Costa Rica.

○ With any type of park in Costa Rica, please make sure to arrive early. This is a country with many tourists, so things get packed super easily. It's best to arrive right when a location opens. This is especially true if you really want to enjoy a park, or see animals early in the morning. Also, make sure you make reservations in advance if the park allows.

● Attend the Café Monteverde Farm & Roastery Tour

○ This one's for those who love going through foodie experiences. This tour covers the start to finish of the coffee-making process. Based on testimonials, it seems like visitors are fascinated by the sustainable approach taken by the farm.

● Go Birdwatching for Hummingbirds

○ How cute are hummingbirds? There are about 300 species of them; about 50 of them can be found right in Costa Rica! Selvatura Park has a hummingbird garden where you're able to see them up close and personal. This is truly a once-in-a-lifetime opportunity!

Where to Stay:

- Outbox Inn Hostel
  - This is a popular hostel that seems to pop up all over TikTok when you're planning a trip to Monteverde.

- Hotel Belmar
  - A sunset happy hour AND a vegetable patch for fresh produce?! This hotel seems to have it all!

- Hotel Poco a Poco

Where and What to Eat:

- San Lucas Treetop Dining Experience
  - If you're feeling a bit bougie, please be sure to check out this restaurant as it's truly unlike any other! Some of the dishes you'll receive are interactive, and just have a look at their Instagram to see how the tables are set up.

- The Open Kitchen

- Panaderia Jimenez

How to Get Around:

- To get around in Monteverde, most people walk or take taxis. This is also one of the towns that has Uber in Costa Rica, so yet another great option.

LA FORTUNA

La Fortuna is located about 2.5 hours north of San José and is considered one of the most popular destinations in Costa Rica.

Things to Do:

- Hike Arenal Volcano

  ○ Recognized as Costa Rica's best-known volcano, Arenal Volcano is one that you cannot miss. Seriously. You look out, and it's right in plain sight! Most people do recognize Costa Rica for its biodiversity and as a leader in ecotourism. While many people may want to relax from their busy 9–5 lives, others may want to throw on their hiking boots and explore. There are about 8 hiking trails that you could possibly go on, but many visitors decide to take the Main Lookout route where in addition to the breathtaking view, you can see some lava flow remains—how amazing does that sound?! As a note, the volcano is active, but it has not erupted since 2010.

● Experience a Magical Waterfall

○ You can't leave without visiting La Fortuna Waterfall. It is one of the most visited waterfalls in Costa Rica. In fact, waterfalls are a must in any Latin American country. Costa Rica's rich tropical landscape is the perfect home for lush and magical cascades. Once you take the trek to the waterfalls, you'll be able to spend time in the water enjoying the landscape around you and capture great content for your TikTok account.

○ Now that you have these adventurous opportunities in mind, here are some items that you would need to bring along with you to fully enjoy the experience.

■ Hiking shoes

● This is pretty self-explanatory. Sneakers can work as well, especially if you don't want the hiking shoes to take up a huge portion of your luggage.

■ Strong-grip sandals

- Sandals are highly recommended, especially when you're near the waterfall. You don't want to get your sneakers wet, so it's always good to have a pair of sandals in your bag.

■ Rain jacket

- Since it is a tropical country, the weather can be quite unpredictable. A small raincoat is always something good to carry around.

■ Mini first-aid kit

- This is something that everyone should have on any hike, especially if they're not in their home country. You're not familiar with the area so you're not sure where the nearest hospital is.

■ Mosquito repellent

- The mosquitos are ruthless, especially if you're not used to that type of tropical environment. If you don't want to use the spray repellent, there are also bracelets that repel mosquitos.

  - Sunscreen

  - Bathing suit

- El Salto Rope Swing

  ○ If you're still craving adventure, then this is right up your alley! A couple of minutes away (by walking) from the downtown area and under the bridge by Road 702, you'll see El Salto Rope Swing. If you feel confident enough, then go ahead and take your swing. It's also entertaining to watch people do the brave activity.

Where to Stay:

- Selina La Fortuna

  ○ Throughout this guide, you'll see a couple of mentions of Selina hostels. You'll find these hostels throughout many Latin

American countries, but they are expanding into other parts of the world. Selinas are famous for their CoLive program, which means that you can sign up for a package to stay at the many locations for a certain price. Also, this hostel chain is great for digital nomads, given that they have well-known coworking spaces with super-fast Wi-Fi. They typically also have workout equipment.

● Amor Arenal

  ○ Located in a rainforest, this hotel is truly a dream come true! It consists of bungalows and has multiple pools with swim-up bars.

● The Springs

  ○ This luxurious resort includes natural hot and cold springs, a full-service spa, and an amazing view of the beautiful Arenal Volcano. Highly recommended if there's more flexibility in your travel budget.

Where and What to Eat:

● Tierra Mia Restaurante

- [Restaurante La Parada](#)

- Tiquicia Restaurant

How to Get Around:

- Many travelers decide to rent a scooter or a bicycle during their time in La Fortuna. Vehicle rental locations are distributed throughout the location.

TAMARINDO

Let's start making our way to the North Pacific coast for Tamarindo. It's a small beach town with just so much to do!

*"Tamarindo" is a tropical fruit that is very popular throughout Latin America. Might as well try some if you end up visiting!

Things to Do:

- Go Surfing and Shred the Nar!

  - It is no secret that Costa Rica is a popular destination for surfers. Whether you're a beginner or an expert, surfing in Costa Rica is a must. If you do end up spending time around the coast, you'll encounter many laid-back surf towns, Playa Tamarindo being one of the leading areas for this sport. The waves are about 3–5 feet, making them perfect for any level of surf that you may be on. Playa Tamarindo is also home to a variety of surfing schools and camps. The prices vary depending on how long you want to take the lessons, whether you want to take private or group classes, etc. Since Costa Rica's weather is pretty stagnant, the Pacific coast is pretty dependable for surfing during any time of the year.

○ Some recommended surf schools are:

- ■ Iguana Surf Camp and Lodging

- ■ Surf Ranch Tamarindo

- ■ Surf Spirit Costa Rica

○ If you're wondering whether or not to bring a surfboard with you for surf camp, you don't really have to. Surf camp is for all levels so some people may bring their own board, but camps will typically provide these for you. Instead, focus on bringing the following:

- ■ Swimwear

  - ● This can be a bathing suit. Your surf camp will most likely provide a body suit, but you can of course bring your own.

- Reusable water bottle

  - We'll get into how you can be an eco-friendly tourist toward the end of the guide, but make sure to bring your own reusable water bottle, especially the ones that can keep your drink cool. Also, bringing a plastic bottle will risk adding plastic to the beautiful Costa Rican beaches.

- Beach bag

  - Make sure you bring everything you need with you in your bag. You never know if you make new friends at surf camp and you guys want to go for lunch afterwards. You'll need your wallet and a place to put your wet clothes.

- ■ Sunglasses

- ■ Sun hat

- ■ Sunscreen

● Go Canyoneering

  ○ Canyoneering is also a great option for adventurous souls. If you don't know what this is, it's basically climbing up a canyon or a mountain (in the case of Costa Rica, through waterfalls as well) through different, strategic techniques. It's for those who are looking for an extra boost of adrenaline in their trip. The places in which you're able to engage in this activity as a tourist are Tamarindo, South Pacific, Manuel Antonio, Monteverde, and Arenal Volcano.

● Visit the Monkey Park

  ○ When people visit Costa Rica, they expect to see many animals. You do encounter a lot of wildlife on hikes, and you can also see them in sanctuaries and shelters. The Monkey Park is a great place to see a variety of animals in their new environment. This is also a very fun place for kids if you're visiting with a family.

- Take a Walk along Playa Conchal

  ○ Don't feel the need to be consistently doing something while traveling. A major goal of any journey is being able to experience the country. If you want to lay on the beach and experience a Costa Rican beach, that's absolutely fine!

Where to Stay:

- Les Voiles Blanches

  ○ This boutique hotel will have you in awe! The aesthetics are beautiful, and it's situated in the perfect area.

- Wyndham Tamarindo Resort

  ○ Believe it or not, many Tamarindo visitors really enjoy staying at the Wyndham in Tamarindo. It has great amenities and very easy access to shuttles to go off and participate in excursions.

- Selina Tamarindo

Where and What to Eat:

- Fish and Cheeses

○ I know what you're thinking. Italian cuisine in Costa Rica? This happens to be a tourist favorite and the go-to spot for some comfort pasta. They even make their cheese fresh on a daily basis. The Italian-owned location also caters to special events, so if you're looking to have a birthday dinner, this would be the spot!

● El Vaquero with Volcano Brewing

○ You're probably wondering what "Volcano Brewing" is, and so did we when we first came across this restaurant. Located in *Witch's Rock Surf Camp*, El Vaquero is a family-friendly beach hangout spot with its own brewery. This location has many great events for you to get to know travelers and try the "Volcano Brewing" for yourself.

● Pangas Beach Club

○ Fresh food awaits at Pangas Beach Club! This restaurant seems to be a favorite among TikTok vloggers for its elegant location and decadent meals. It's perfect for lounging on the beach with some friends and having a classy time at night. Plus, it's a pet-friendly location!

How to Get Around:

- Since Tamarindo is small, you can get to many places by renting a bike or a motorcycle. If you want to do day trips elsewhere (and this will apply to all locations listed in this guide), you can book a shuttle.

SANTA TERESA

Another small town that seems to be getting a lot of attention now is Santa Teresa. Located further south than Tamarindo, this is a great location for digital nomads.

If you're out early in the morning (let's say around 6 a.m.), and you're on the street curve around Nantipa, you can see some spider monkeys on the cable wires, headed to the greenery. This is truly such a calming element of nature to watch, especially without people on the streets.

Things to Do:

- Take a Day Trip to Isla Tortuga

  ○ Costa Rica has many beautiful islands, and while you're in Santa Teresa, you might as well go and explore this one! It's the perfect location for a day trip with friends since there are many fun, water-related activities to do there. Some things that you could possibly do are snorkeling, kayaking, and setting up your own barbecue by the beach.

50

- Go Surfing

  - Since this town is smaller and a little less well known than other places near the Pacific coast, it is a bit easier to book a class and have more room for your surfing lessons. This is great for anyone who is a beginner and would like more one-on-one time with instructors.

- See the Montezuma Waterfalls

  - About 40 minutes from Santa Teresa are the Montezuma Waterfalls. So there are three waterfalls here and require a short hike (about a 40-minute walk). Some people say that the path is a little bit unclear at times, so if you feel better traveling with a group to avoid confusion, that would be ideal. The best part is that the entrance is free.

- View the Sunset at Vista de Olas

  - If you're looking for the best view in Santa Teresa, definitely visit the Sunset Lounge Hotel. Once you're there, you can order a drink at the bar and that's where you'll see the gorgeous sunset (and trust us when we say that Pacific sunsets are 100% worth it). Plus, you'll be able to swim in the infinity pool!

Where to Stay:

- Selina (South)

  ○ We'll mention Selina here once again because it truly has such an amazing community. Plus, it does tend to get booked very quickly, just like the coworking space does. It's a really nice space to work and has super-fast Wi-Fi like most Selinas, but if you're looking to stay or work here, make sure that you reserve far in advance.

- Vista del Alma

  ○ This boutique hotel has probably one of the most magical views in Santa Teresa. It is meant for those with a higher budget. Please keep in mind that it is not all-inclusive.

- House of Somos

  ○ This one's for all the surfers looking for community!

Where and What to Eat:

- Eat Street

  - If you can't decide on what to eat, then this street food marketplace should be your first stop. They have a variety of food for you to try and ample space for you to bring along a big group of friends.

- The Bakery

  - If you're walking along Santa Teresa, you're going to see a pastel pink place named, "The Bakery" that is ALWAYS packed with people. Now don't let the name fool you. This place does have an abundance of decadent baked goods, but they also have salads, pastas, sandwiches, and so much more. Definitely worth a visit and a cute vlog!

- Good Munchies

  - Let's say you're coming from the beach and want something quick yet filling. This Venezuelan cafe is the perfect spot for you then. They have smoothies, arepas, and so many more delicious Venezuelan foods.

- Pizza Tomate

○ Picture this: it's a rainy day and you're finished with all your activities. There's nothing much else to do but wind down in your hotel room. But you're craving something comforting to fill you up for the night. Most restaurants are closed, except for this pizza place. You check it out and are immediately swooped in by the aroma of fresh tomato sauce and warm bread. Pizza Tomate is definitely THE comfort food spot that you need to try when you're in Santa Teresa.

How to Get Around:

● This is one of the locations where there is a lot of dirt instead of pavement. Renting a bike may be the economical option, but an ATV, motorcycle, or electric scooter are all better options. Trust us, they will especially come in handy when it rains. A popular location to rent is Savannah Xtreme Tours Atv Rental.

JACO

A bit larger than Tamarindo, Jaco gives off the same hostel and nightlife energy. It's a great destination for backpackers and digital nomads.

Things to Do:

● Visit Parque Nacional Manuel Antonio

○ About an hour and a half away from Jaco is a 16 square kilometer park called Parque Nacional Manuel Antonio. It may be one of Costa Rica's smallest national parks, but there's so much to do and see!

■ Go Paddle Boarding

● If you prefer not to get soaked by the waves from surfing, then paddle boarding is a great option for you. Just like many other locations in Costa Rica, this park offers paddle boarding options for visitors. You can either do it standing up or kneeled, and it does require that balance that you get from surfing. Also, did you know that you can do yoga while paddle boarding?! Schools like Bob Marley Surf School offer group sessions where you'll be able to paddle board into the sunset with your friends. You're certainly going to want to experience that!

■ Take a Tour with a Naturalist

● Since this park is a bit smaller than the others in the country, you have a better chance of encountering the beautiful wildlife. It's even better to walk along the park with a tour guide that can spot out animals and plants way easier than you could probably do so (unless you're an expert yourself). The price for this guide ranges from $60–$80 USD per person and takes about 3 hours.

● Visit Parque Nacional Carara

○ Another national park that is about a 30-minute drive from Jaco is Carara. This is truly a bird lover's paradise. You'll see a variety of wildlife of course, but many people go to see the different bird species. This is also a spot for many school field trips, so be prepared for many group tours when you arrive.

● Experience Jaco's Popular Nightlife

   ○ Jaco used to be such a calm beach town, and now it's known as the party capital of Costa Rica! You'll see many bachelorette parties, locals coming in from San José, and backpackers from all over coming to join the party scene.

● Visit El Miro

   ○ Since you're on the west coast, you might as well try and get the best view of the sunset. El Miro is an observation deck located just a couple of minutes from the center of Jaco and is recommended to go walking with friends. There are also pretty murals and graffiti there for you to see. Many people do this as a form of exercise, especially if they're staying in Jaco for an extended period of time. Plus, it's free.

● Attend a Wellness Retreat

   ○ Costa Rica is known to nourish the soul with its luxurious natural surroundings. This is the go-to destination for people who want a spiritual cleanse or who are interested in getting more in tune with themselves. Check out this great wellness retreat that is only about an hour and a half drive from Jaco:

- Finca de Vida

● This center is all about a journey to wellness through healing foods. During your time there, you'll have a cleanse, participate in demos, practice some yoga, and most importantly, heal. It's all about a vacation for health at Finca de Vida. What's even more cool is that you'll be on a "Farm of Life" and go through a tasty raw food detox.

● A quick tip for these wellness retreats. Sometimes, you can't automatically join them by just paying for your stay. You will have to set up a call with one of the mediators to see if their specific retreat is right for you. These are more common in retreats that are more spirituality-based. So be sure to call the center you want to attend to guarantee your entry.

● Wellness centers in Costa Rica do cost money, depending on how long you want to stay and what you decide to do. You can stay for a day or a month, but many people choose to be there for about a week. Here are some items you may need to bring along if you decide to stay during this 7-day period:

- **Yoga Clothes**

○ Make sure that you bring enough comfortable clothing for however long you are staying. Please keep in mind that they may not have washing machines so your clothes may be washed through a shorter process, such as handwashing.

- **A Couple of Sweaters**

○ Depending on the time that you go and how high up the center is (wellness retreats are usually isolated and elevated to have nicer views of nature), it may get a bit chilly at night. Be sure to have the proper clothing.

- **Journal and a Pen**

○ This is a beautiful time for self-reflection. Many retreats will have workshops to just write and reflect.

- ● Book(s)
  - ○ There's a 10/10 chance that you won't be able to use your phone or laptop during your retreat. Be sure to bring books for when you have some down time.

- ● Swimwear
  - ○ Many of these retreats will have you go into the mystical cascades of Costa Rica, so be prepared.

Where to Stay:

- ● Quick tip: If you're looking to have the full Jaco experience, it's recommended to stay in a hostel. In addition to making new friends, you'll be near the nightlife and be close to many attractions.

- ● Selina Jacó Beach Hotel
  - ○ This has to be one of the cooler looking Selinas! You've probably seen some TikToks of the cool pods that they have!

- ● Room2Board
  - ○ Another surf school located in a hostel? Sign us up! Room2Board is a boutique

hostel, meaning that it may be a bit more pricier than the regular hostel.

- Diamante del Sol 801S

  ○ If you're looking for a vacation condo for a group of people, this place is perfect for you! Quick tip—it's significantly cheaper to book on Booking.com than Airbnb.

Where and What to Eat:

- Ryana

  ○ The food and vibes here are immaculate! Definitely worth visiting!

- El Pelicano

  ○ This restaurant has delicious food and a great dining experience. It's really fun if you go with a big group of friends!

- Bowie's Point Bar & Restaurant

- Koko Gastro Bar

- Mahi Mahi Chill Out Restaurant

How to Get Around:

- In Jaco, you can walk, rent a bike or scooter. Although, this is a bigger town than some that we have mentioned, so you'll probably have to take a taxi every once in a while. A typical fare back to your accommodation would be around 2055 CRC.

PUERTO JIMÉNEZ

There are just too many great things to be said about this region to not include it in this travel guide!

Things to Do:

● Walk along the Corcovado National Park

○ Let's start off with the biggest national park in Costa Rica. The Corcovado National Park is located on the southern Pacific end of the country. Fun fact—this park is just one of the few sizable areas of lowland rainforest still in the world. There are many hikes that you can take in this park, but the most popular one is from Leona to Sirena which should take about 5 hours. If you're looking for a shorter trip to squeeze other activities into your schedule, then La Leona Madrigal Trail is perfect for you considering that it only takes about 3 hours to complete. If you're looking for a hike that is a bit more extensive, consider spending the night at Sirena Ranger Station. This is a wooden cabin that is connected to a variety of trails. Many travelers decide to stop here for a night and continue their trek to experience more of the diverse wildlife. In fact, according to "Much Better Adventures," the National Geographic named the place, "the most biologically intense place on Earth in terms of biodiversity."

- Go through a Spiritual Transformation for the Luna Lodge

  ○ Located on the Osa Peninsula and overlooking Corcovado National Park, is a wellness ecolodge. Luna Lodge is surrounded by nature all around and allows their guests to immerse themselves in multiple wellness activities. For instance, you're able to go stargazing, go on a self-guided tour, swim in freshwater, and more. A really interesting activity is the Luna Lodge Full Moon Experience. Visitors can get in tune with the lunar cycle and connect with themselves in a completely different way.

- Watch Dolphins and Whales

  ○ Golfo Dulce (aka "sweet gulf") is perfect for anyone looking to take a glance at the marine life. There are people who usually go whale watching around July to

September. You can also go scuba diving if you're brave enough!

- Take a Chocolate Tour at Rancho Raices de Osa

  - This one's for the foodies! Rancho Raices de Osa has such amazing reviews. People are really interested in the farming practices and the chocolate making process at the end of the tour. It's perfect for traveling families.

Where to Stay:

- Bolita Rainforest Hostel

  - If you want to know what it feels like to be in the middle of a rainforest, this hostel will definitely help you accomplish that. It's a low-impact hostel, meaning that it's run by solar panels and batteries. Please note that this is a naturalist hostel.

- Lapa Rios Lodge

  - You're going to encounter an abundant amount of wildlife anywhere that you go in Costa Rica, but this lodge will truly show it all! You'll encounter endangered monkeys, bird species you've never seen before, and more. It's a really nice stay!

- Iguana Lodge

  ○ Many tourists tend to stay in this hotel.

Where and What to Eat:

- Since it is a small area, you can find many local vendors. Some tourist-favorite restaurants are:

  ○ Pearl of the Osa

    ■ This is near Iguana Lodge if you decide to take up the recommendation. It's sophisticated dining with a very extensive menu.

  ○ Restaurante Carolina

    ■ If you're looking for something a bit more authentic, Restaurante Carolina is where it's at! There are many different kinds of food here including fresh smoothies.

How to Get Around:

- You can honestly explore the entire town by bike since it is a very small area.

PUERTO VIEJO

Let's make our way over to the Caribbean coast to the laid-back town of Puerto Viejo. This is usually the first stop for people that cross the border from Panama, and a town that you just can't skip over.

Quick tip: If you're looking to socialize and make new friends, this may not be the place for you. Of course, you'll talk to people and gain friendships anywhere you go, but people here are a bit more calmer than usual. For instance, reception at many of the hotels are pretty much nonexistent. They will check you in, but you'll probably be surrounded by silence in hotel lobbies.

Things to Do:

- Take Yoga Classes

  - There's just something so relaxing about the Caribbean coast of Costa Rica. This is where you'll find many calming activities, such as yoga and Pilates. Here are some great locations for these types of classes:

    - AmaSer

    - AmaSer is a cafe and yoga center that makes you feel like you're in the clouds. Seriously. To get to the center, you have to take a trip uphill, and you'll find an isolated cafe. While there, you'll be able to purchase vegan baked goods and meet new people. If you walk up the stairs, there will be smiling faces, a yoga center with mats, body pillows, and just so much open space. They offer a variety of classes that cater to all your mindful needs.

- **■** Classes at Hostels

- **●** As previously mentioned, we know that hostels are great options for solo travelers, but did you know that they also offer amazing yoga classes? For instance, at the Selina in Puerto Viejo, they offer yoga classes every morning for those staying at the hostel and for those staying elsewhere. They offer yoga mats, blocks, and amazing yoga instructors. Zeneidas Surf Garden is also a hostel that offers great chant sessions, where you're able to meet people, meditate, and sing songs together. They usually offer these closer to the nighttime. It's truly a great experience and will probably convince you to stay in Costa Rica longer.

- **■** Costa Rica is also well-known for having amazing yoga instructors and facilities in the middle of rainforests. I mean, think about the last time you saw a POV on TikTok of a freelancer.

They wake up, show you their breakfast, and then the casual yoga mat surrounded by lush greenery. If you feel like that's more of your vibe, then these yoga retreats are for you.

- Enjoy a Spa Day

  - You're on vacation so might as well enjoy pampering yourself! PURE Jungle Spa has massages, facials, and so many more relaxing practices.

- Explore the Underwater

  - While many people enjoy the biodiversity on land, there is still much more to discover under the water. Snorkeling adventures are common in the country on both the Caribbean and Pacific sides. The Gandoca Manzanillo Wildlife Refuge is considered to be one of the best spots to go snorkeling. The waters in this area are calm and great for those looking to explore what's beneath the surface. In fact, many visitors do prefer the eastern coast for snorkeling rather than the west, which has more waves and is better suited for surfing.

○ If you're wondering what to bring with you for going scuba diving abroad, bring what you would typically bring to a beach day. The park or tour company that you decide to go with will provide you with all the necessary equipment.

○ We want to make a separate note about protecting the coral reefs. At the end of this guide, we'll talk about environmental impact, but for now, we will advise to please bring eco-friendly sunscreen. This is of course safer for biodiversity underwater. Also, this sunscreen should be worn whenever you're going to a beach, especially if you're just a visitor.

● Take a Guided Tour

○ As you wander around Puerto Viejo, you'll see many travel agencies with different excursions. This is a nice idea if you're looking for a change to your routine.

Where to Stay:

● Cabinas Montesol

○ We cannot emphasize how great and extremely clean this family-owned hotel is. Prices are fair for the area. Plus, if you're sharing a bathroom, trust us when we say that it's constantly cleaned and very spacious. Plus, their two dogs are super friendly and adorable!

- Casa Wolaba

  ○ Casa Wolaba is a fun and very social hostel. It's the perfect place to make travel buddies! Also, they have air conditioning in every room.

- Hotel Aguas Claras

  ○ This cute, boutique hotel is located steps away from the beach. It's a really nice tropical getaway for those looking for that kind of vibe.

- Le Caméléon

  ○ This is a luxury hotel that has come up way too many times on our Instagram feeds. It has wooden panels, rainfall showerheads, and beach access. It's more of a resort experience than anything.

- Shawandha Lodge

  ○ Wooden bungalows galore at Shawandha Lodge! This is for people that truly just want to relax and enjoy a relaxing vacation. Everything you need is either in the lodge or very close by.

Where and What to Eat:

- Restaurante Riquísimo

  - The name says it all! This is the perfect place for lunch or dinner. Plus, you HAVE to try their coconut rice. It's the best in town!

- Pizzeria Dalilí

  - If you couldn't tell from this travel guide so far, we are obsessed with pizza as comfort food, haha!

- Stashu's Con Fusion

  - It is sometimes rare to find brunch out of the states, and this place serves it for you! It's a beachfront location that's perfect for you and your friends.

- Bread & Chocolate

  - Now don't be fooled by the name because this isn't a bakery. Bread & Chocolate is a breakfast and lunch restaurant that offers such amazing food! This tends to be a popular spot for many tourists.

How to Get Around:

- When you arrive, you'll see many people riding their mopeds or bikes. We will say that there are many curves on the roads, and the cars and trucks do come in pretty quickly. It's best to go through the road without headphones in.

CAHUITA

Looking for a small, quiet, relaxing beach community? Then Cahuita is perfect for you! It's also way less busy than Puerto Viejo.

Things to Do:

- Visit the Parque Nacional de Cahuita

  ○ You simply cannot leave this town without visiting its national park. Something that differentiates it from the other parks that we've mentioned is that it is best known for its coral reefs. It's best to visit during the dry season because the park can potentially close down due to flooding or rainfall.

  ○ Something quite beautiful about this park are the sandy white beaches. It honestly looks like you're walking on loads and loads of sugar.

- ○ Also, there's no need to reserve in advance to visit the park. You can just go in once you pay for entrance.

- Check out the Old Reef Farm

  - ○ Remember when we mentioned that there are SO many different fruits in Costa Rica? Well, now is your chance to try them all! There are hundreds of different fruits—like HUNDREDS! This is definitely a great stop on your trip.

- See Sloths at the Sloth Sanctuary of Costa Rica

  - ○ This one is pretty self-explanatory. If you would like to see rescued sloths, then this is your opportunity.

Where to Stay:

- Casa de las Flores Boutique Hotel

  - ○ There are many limited accommodation options in this area since it is so small, but this boutique hotel seems to be the most popular option.

- 3 Bamboo Ecolodge

  - ○ We love a nice ecolodge! You have the option to stay in either a villa or treehouse—how cool is that?!

- [The Goddess Garden Eco Resort](#)

    - This is more of a retreat, but still an amazing option to stay at!

Where and What to Eat:

- El Purgatorio Bar & Restaurant

    - A bar and restaurant with great seafood and awesome vibes!

- El Cangrejo Loco de Cahuita

- El Rincón del Amor

How to Get Around:

- Cahuita is honestly such a laid-back, small area. Most people just prefer to walk to get from place to place.

TORTUGUERO

"Tortuga" in Spanish means "turtle," so expect to see the cute animals there. Tortuguero is a very popular location in Costa Rica and tends to have many volunteers from all over the world (volunteer opportunities will be presented toward the end of this travel guide).

Things to Do:

- Walk Around Tortuguero Village

○ Upon arriving in the Tortuguero region, many people immediately head to the park and forget about this colorful town! There are many street vendors throughout the town that offer nice prices on fruits and handcrafted goods.

● Check out all that there is to do at the Tortuguero National Park

○ Visit the Sea Turtle Conservancy

■ Tortuguero National Park is the most important site for sea turtle nesting in the world. This is probably one of the first stops you should do considering all that you're going to be seeing in the park. The workers and volunteers provide such helpful information surrounding turtles and the park in general.

○ Go on a Night Walk in the Rainforest

■ To do this, you're going to need to book with a company (this can also be booked through the hotel you're staying at). From there, guides will pick you up and take you into the park late at night.

From there, they'll be able to show you all the wildlife that shows up like snakes, frogs, etc.

○ Go White Water Rafting

■ You can do almost every activity with a group of friends, but white water rafting has to be one of the top choices for group activities! Just imagine navigating fast waters on an inflatable raft with the people you just met at your hostel. How fun and chaotic does that sound? This park and the Pacuare River are nice spots for white water rafting that offer many tours for people at all levels.

■ In terms of packing for white water rafting, it would be:

● Bathing suit

● Breathable clothes

● Sneakers

● Water shoes

● Plastic zip-up bag for phone

○ Depending on the level of white water rafting, you may be able to bring your phone to capture some fun images!

● For the rest of the items (like helmet, etc.), remember that there are opportunities to rent certain equipment and gear.

● Go Turtle Watching

○ The activity you've been waiting for—the turtles in Tortuguero! As a note, any time you want to specifically see wildlife in Costa Rica, make sure that it is with a tour guide. Remember that they are the experts, meaning that they know the best time to see them, how close you should get to the animals, and all of the small details that you may not have even thought of. As soon as you arrive in Tortuguero, you're immediately going to see travel companies talk to you about booking a time to see the turtles. So, we recommend going with any of these people.

○ In terms of timing for those who specifically want to see the green sea turtles during their visit to Costa Rica, the best time to go is between July and August. Nesting season is usually between July–October, so keep that in mind for turtle visits.

Where to Stay:

● <u>Hotel El Icaco</u>

○ This place is just a few steps from the beach and surrounded by the beauty of Costa Rica's nature.

● <u>Mawamba Lodge</u>

● <u>Pachira Lodge</u>

Where and What to Eat:

● Taylor's Place Tortuguero Costa Rica

● Budda Cafe

● Tutti's Pizzeria y Restaurante

How to Get Around:

● In full transparency, you're going to find yourself in a boat the majority of the time due to the area's location. People that stay in town usually just walk or take their bikes along with them.

WHAT NOT TO
DO IN COSTA RICA

We've provided you with a pretty thorough list of things to do in Costa Rica. Here's some advice on things to not do, for your reference:

● Do Not Smoke in Costa Rica

   ○ Didn't think of this one, did you? Costa Rica is joining many other Latin American countries in being a smoke-free country. This is in an effort to protect public health. This includes no smoking in every place you go to including workspaces, bus stops, bars, and all of the others.

● Do Not Try and See the Entire Country in One Trip

○ As you can see, there's just so much to do in Costa Rica! The guide above is even just a recommended list, so there is still another entire adventure in the country for you to enjoy. Just like any other country, it is a lot to see. In fact, Costa Rica is 19,700 square miles. Don't pressure yourself to see everything at once and soak in whichever areas that you can. Costa Rica will always be there for you to visit.

● Do Not Immediately Make the Move to Costa Rica

○ When some people visit the country, they fall in love with its beauty and just want to move there. We 100% understand that free-spirited urge. Our recommendation is to hold on to your dream for just a little bit longer and do a couple of trial runs in the country. Remember that you probably came on vacation so you're seeing such a small portion of the country. Take an ample amount of time to see different areas and then determine if you would like to live there long-term.

● Do Not See the Wildlife on your Own

○ Ok—this one's a bit odd to state because there's wildlife all over the country. You will encounter them on walks and on some excursions, but please do not take it past that. Instead, if you want to see some animals, be sure to have a tour guide with you. They are the animal experts and know how to deal with the animals. Also, please do not take photos with the animals (as this encourages photo tourism) and do not feed them (we don't want them to be reliant on human food).

● Do Not Avoid the Country Because of Rainy Season

○ As we know, the rainy season is typically from May to December. Hearing the word "rain" may ruin any vacation plans for people who usually want to relax in the sunshine. Again, the country is just so vibrant during this time, and you'll experience nature like you never have. Plus, this is a tropical country, and the same exact weather can be expected of any other place with the same climate. All of these countries have methods of continuing activities with or without rain. For instance, in Costa Rica, there are umbrellas at outdoor-seating restaurants, and tour guides are equipped with additional raincoats just in case the water hits at any minute. Plus, you'll get tours at a cheaper discount during the rainy season. Doesn't get any better than that!

- Do Not Rent a Car to Travel the Country

  ○ We can guarantee that driving in your home country does not equate to driving in any other country. It's recommended to take a public bus or private shuttle to go from place to place. It's a faster option and usually comes out so much cheaper. Plus, there are just so many traffic laws to obey in Costa Rica, so you may make a mistake and get easily fined. For example, how are you supposed to know that you're not supposed to pass through an area with yellow lines?

- Do Not Assume that Everyone Knows English

  ○ As mentioned at the beginning of the guide, Spanish is Costa Rica's national language. Even though it is a tourist destination, and many people know English, it is still expected of you to know the basics. This is why it's important to just take the time to learn the basics of a language. If you have language confidence issues, don't worry about that at all. It's completely normal and they know that you're a tourist trying to navigate the country and be a global citizen.

- Do Not Let the Idea of "Traveling by Yourself" Stop You from Going to Costa Rica

  ○ Let's face it—group trips rarely make it out of the chat. You all get super excited about the possibility of going somewhere. Then, when it's time to plan, everyone decides to ghost one another. "Oh, it's just not possible with work now!" "Ugh, this falls on my cousin's wedding! So sorry!" We've all heard those excuses (and maybe even created some ourselves), and it just ruins the whole travel high. You may have to do some trips on your own and that's *totally okay*. Solo traveling is such a fun experience and you're spending time with the best person on the planet—yourself.

  ○ In terms of solo traveling in Costa Rica, just do it. Many people actually choose Costa Rica as their first country to travel on their own. You'll be safe as long as you're aware of your surroundings (like anywhere else in the world) and you'll make SO many friends at hostels, so you'll never feel lonely. Take that leap and plan the solo trip!

BE CONSCIOUS OF YOUR ENVIRONMENTAL IMPACT

While Costa Rica is a country full of vast landscapes, it is important that we preserve its beauty. One of the key takeaways from traveling to Costa Rica should be an awakening to the beauty of nature and how we must protect her at all costs. In fact, Costa Rica leaves people wanting to stay immersed in nature, but just remember some key factors about its beautiful environment. Anyone can help in the conservation of the ecosystem in Costa Rica. You can be a tourist and still be able to provide assistance to the country's beauty. This is called Eco-tourism. It's tourism that is used to aid a threatened ecosystem. Here are some key takeaways that you could incorporate in the country and in your daily life:

● **Don't Take Pictures with the Animals**

○ We know that cute sloths and a variety of wildlife are in Costa Rica, but they are not meant for pictures. This easily turns into photo tourism and encourages people to open unethical animal facilities. Friendly reminder that animals want to be in nature, away from humans. It's fine to take a picture of an animal, but it should not have you or anyone else in it.

● **Drive Less**

○ Driving is harmful to any environment because of the harmful gasses it gives off. This gas is called greenhouse gasses. These gasses are dangerous for our health and for the planet. Burning gasoline causes the production of nitrogen dioxide, carbon monoxide, hydrocarbons, benzene, and formaldehyde.

○ To avoid driving, it is recommended that you take the buses or ride a bike. Riding a bike is so much more beneficial for the environment since it does not burn gasoline. Biking around can also be a fun experience since you're breathing in the fresh air and taking in that beautiful view of Costa Rica. You may also get a good workout in. Back in your home country, you may not have a great public transportation system and it may be more commonly used to use a car. In that case, make sure to carpool as often as you can.

● **Limit your Water Usage**

  ● Do not use unnecessary water if you're trying to be eco-friendly. The water we use comes from natural rivers, run-offs, and oceans. The more water we use, the more energy will be used to collect more water which burns more fuel.

  ● To avoid wasting water, take shorter showers. Showering takes a lot of water; shortening that time will make a huge difference on the amount of water you use. Make sure to turn off the faucet when you're brushing your teeth or washing your hands.

● **Use Less Plastic**

  ○ The production of plastic is dangerous for the environment because it uses energy from fossil fuels which creates the harmful gasses. Using plastic will increase its demand, which means companies will start producing more.

○ To prevent using a lot of plastic, consider using reusable shopping bags or refillable water bottles. We've mentioned reusable water bottles a couple of times in this travel guide. It's truly a small step like this that can have a tremendous impact on the environment.

● **Educate Yourself and Others**

○ Collectively, if everyone participates in eco-tourism, we can make a huge difference. Let your friends and family know, and share your ideas.

○ Also, when you leave Costa Rica, be sure to mention the biodiversity and sustainability efforts you witnessed to friends and family to build awareness.

● Speaking of education, here are some facts about Costa Rica's conservation to help educate others:

○ Costa Rica is the first country in the world to fix their deforestation problem.

■ Costa Rica was able to slow down their tree chopping activities, and instead use it to grow trees. Since 1990, Costa Rica's tree population has tripled!

○ 30% of Costa Rica's oceans are protected.

○ By 2025, Costa Rica will have protected all of their wetlands.

  ■ They also plan to increase the area size of the wetlands by at least 10% by 2030.

If you still want to learn more, here are some great resources:

● *The Nature Dilemma - Costa Rica's Bet on Humanity: The Green Nation's (successful) Blueprint for Climate Action & Marine Protection – Now*

○ This podcast goes into a deeper dive of Costa Rica and its success story of being a global climate leader.

● *The Ecolaboratory: Environmental Governance and Economic Development in Costa Rica* by Robert Fletcher

○ A book that goes into a deeper dive into Costa Rica's environmental policies.

ADIOS, COSTA RICA

I'm sure you won't want to leave Costa Rica, but all trips have to come to an end at some point. For those of you who do not want to leave the beautiful Central American country just yet, consider volunteering. Luckily, Costa Rica does have wildlife conservations that are always looking for volunteers. Please see some great options below:

GoEco - Sea Turtle Conservation

Location: Talamanca

Overview: This volunteer organization allows you to preserve sea turtles by patrolling the beach, protecting eggs by taking them to a hatchery, keeping the beaches clean, etc. On top of this, you will also have accommodation, free meals, and more. You can also add Spanish classes to your experience.

Jaguar Rescue Center

Location: Limón, Punta Cocles

Overview: The Jaguar Rescue Center is all about helping injured animals and returning them back to the wild. This is the perfect opportunity for people who would like a one-on-one experience with animals. The animals that do end up here range from spider monkeys to sloths, and much more (no jaguars, haha). Similar to other volunteer opportunities, this does include accommodation.

Eco-Agriculture Conservation

Location: All over, but recommended in Monteverde

Overview: Ever been interested in learning more and actually cultivating the delicious organic food that you had in Costa Rica? Well, this is the perfect opportunity for you! You'll work with local farmers and learn sustainable farming methods as well as their traditional agricultural techniques.

Additionally, there are many other ways to give back to Costa Rica in a sustainable manner. Worldpackers is a great resource for those who want to explore their different volunteering options. Upon first glance of the opportunities, you can teach surf lessons, teach yoga, work as a waiter at a hostel, etc.

Also, if you're a content creator, you have such an advantage while traveling in general! So many hostels, hotels, tour experiences, etc. are looking for people to just take pictures and videos, and vlog about their experience. There are so many Nano and Micro influencers (so you don't have to have a huge following) on TikTok who stay at hotels in different countries as long as they take a video about their experience. These influencers can also get compensated for their creative services. Depending on following and credibility, these influencers can get paid from $1k and beyond. If you're not someone who likes showing their face on camera and who enjoys more of the behind-the-scenes action, you can do the exact same thing. For example, you can provide a new Airbnb host with your professional photos in exchange for a stay and/or compensation. You can also charge for usage rights (meaning they would have to provide you with free housing or money to use your photos on their website). There are also just so many hostels looking for people to handle social media duties in exchange for a free stay. If you're a content creator and this really appeals to you, we highly advise you to try in Costa Rica. All you would have to do is find places that appeal to you and your creative direction, then send them an email of how you would help with their photography, videography, etc. Trust us when we say that this whole idea of travel content creation will not be going away anytime soon since the influencer world is a billion-dollar industry that continues to grow each and every year.

Also, an influx of health instructors do decide to live in Costa Rica due to an increase in spiritual and wellness retreats. This is a practice that is consistently in need in the country. When you go to Costa Rica, you usually see so many flyers for Pilates, yoga, and meditation classes taught by people who are not locals. It's a great chance to extend your trip a bit longer to determine if you want to live here.

If you're feeling adventurous and want to continue traveling, visiting neighboring countries is always a good idea. Nicaragua and Panama are just a bus ride away, so there's no need to even go to San Jose to catch a flight. See recommendations below:

To get to Nicaragua, you'll probably want to go through the Penas Blancas land border crossing which will get you to San Juan del Sur. You'll spend about $5–$10 to exit Costa Rica and $10–$15 to enter Nicaragua. There is the option to rent a car, but many people decide to just take a bus. Tica Bus and Nica Bus are great options. If you do have a higher travel budget, there are private buses that transport a handful of people across the border. Interbus can take you from Liberia, Costa Rica to San Juan del Sur, Nicaragua at a designated time.

To get to Panama, you will most likely cross the Sixaola border. This is about 40 minutes from Puerto Viejo and can drop you close to Bocas del Toro in Panama. Other border options are Rio Sereno and Paso Canoas. You will spend about $5–$10 to exit Costa Rica, and it is a bit unclear whether there is a fee to enter Panama. But, it is important to have a decent amount of cash handy just in case. You can take public buses, but Caribe Shuttle is a private bus option that works as well.

Also, if you do decide to cross borders on wheels versus flying to an airport, you'll need the following:

- Proof of onward travel. Sometimes this can be overlooked by officials at the border, but remember that not having proof of onward travel/leaving the country can prevent you from entering.

- Have sufficient funds. As you can see, exiting and entering a country do require fees. It's important to have funds in Costa Rican Colones or United States Dollars since the border patrols will not take debit or credit cards. Plus, you won't find an ATM at the border so best to be prepared beforehand.

- Keep your passport handy. You're probably going to be asked for this as soon as you arrive. Please be sure to have copies as well.

- COVID-19 test or a vaccination card. Please make sure that you are aware of the requirements of entering a country. They do differ from country to country and from time to time.

- Have a pen handy. There is a lot of action going on at the border and you'll probably have to fill a form or two out. It's always great to have a pen in your backpack for travel occasions like this.

* If you do decide to take flights, please keep in mind that you will most likely need to fly into the capital cities. This is inconvenient if you're enjoying your stay by one of the

coasts and have to make your way to San Jose for the airport. Plus, if you fly into Panama City, you will have a lot to do, but if you fly into Managua, it is not a tourist-friendly city and you're probably going to have to take a bus ride for a couple of hours to get to the nearest tourist area (Granada).

END

We hope this travel guide either convinced you to go to Costa Rica or made your upcoming trip a bit easier. Costa Rica is truly such a beautiful and unique country. In addition to the amazing biodiversity, this country just shows you how many shades of blue and green there are. Seeing nature at its best and wildlife there is such an amazing thing to see! We hope you can make the visit soon!

REFERENCES

https://www.eater.com/maps/best-restaurants-san-jose-costa-rica

https://www.bookmundi.com/t/day-trips-from-san-jose-costa-rica

https://www.worldometers.info/world-population/costa-rica-population/

https://www.vacationscostarica.com/travel-guide/facts/

https://www.trafalgar.com/real-word/fun-facts-costa-rica-happiest-country/

https://travel.usnews.com/Costa_Rica/Getting_Around/

https://www.lonelyplanet.com/articles/how-to-get-around-costa-rica

https://www.muchbetteradventures.com/magazine/best-hikes-in-costa-rica-8-of-the-best-trekking-routes/

https://jameskaiser.com/costa-rica-guide/parks/corcovado/

https://www.alltrails.com/parks/costa-rica/puntarenas--2/corcovado-national-park

https://www.bookmundi.com/t/arenal-volcano-hike-the-best-trails

https://www.costaricarios.com/snorkeling-in-costa-rica-all-you-need-to-know/

https://costaricaexperts.com/things-to-do/diving-scuba-snorkel/

https://www.entercostarica.com/attractions/things-to-do/canyoneering

https://costaricatravelblog.com/the-best-river-for-rafting-in-costa-rica/

https://www.monteverdeinfo.com/

https://www.cafedemonteverde.com/pages/coffee-tour

https://www.wildjunket.com/things-to-do-in-monteverde-costa-rica/

https://destinationlesstravel.com/puerto-jimenez-costa-rica/

https://mytanfeet.com/costa-rica-national-park/poas-volcano/

https://neverendingeverywhere.wordpress.com/2016/12/07/old-reef-farm-or-try-all-the-tropical-fruits/

https://www.audleytravel.com/us/costa-rica/best-time-to-visit#nov-dec

https://www.vacationscostarica.com/travel-guide/weather/#:~:text=Costa%20Rica%20is%20beautifully%20warm,in%20most%20of%20the%20country

https://www.travelbeginsat40.com/event/limon-carnival-costa-rica/

https://www.statista.com/statistics/977562/costa-rica-leading-source-countries-tourism/

https://www.culturalworld.org/what-are-tropical-countries.htm

https://www.willflyforfood.net/food-in-costa-rica/

https://www.travelawaits.com/2481833/best-types-of-fruit-costa-rica/

https://ticotimes.net/2022/06/14/my-5-favorite-desserts-in-costa-rica-that-you-must-try#:~:text=1.,rich%2C%20creamy%2C%20and%20indulgent.

https://www.fishandcheeses.com/

https://witchsrocksurfcamp.com/el-vaquero-brewpub/

https://www.pangasbeachclubcr.com/

https://www.laidbacktrip.com/posts/costa-rica-to-nicaragua-borders-crossing

https://www.therealdealtours.com/blog/blog/crossing-the-costa-rica-border-into-panama/

https://www.goeco.org/area/volunteer-in-central-america/costa rica/sea-turtle-conservation/

https://www.jaguarrescue.foundation/en-us/SupportUs/Volunteering

https://www.volunteerhq.org/destinations/costa-rica/eco-agriculture-in-san-jose/

https://www.twoweeksincostarica.com/first-time-visit-costa-rica/

https://www.kimkim.com/c/the-best-boutique-hotels-in-puerto-viejo

https://www.saltinourhair.com/costa-rica/tortuguero/

https://costaricadreamadventures.com/best-time-for-turtle-watching-in-tortuguero/

https://www.fodors.com/world/mexico-and-central-america/costa-rica/experiences/news/10-things-not-to-do-in-costa-rica

Made in United States
North Haven, CT
16 April 2023

35526219R00061